# Peterbilt

## The Class of the Industry

Henry Rasmussen

**MBI** Publishing Company

First published in 2001 by MBI Publishing Company, Galtier Plaza, Suite 200, 380 Jackson Street, St. Paul, MN 55101-3885 USA

MBI Publishing Company books are also available at discounts in bulk quantity for industrial or sales-promotional use. For details write to Special Sales Manager at Motorbooks International Wholesalers & Distributors, 729 Prospect Avenue, PO Box 1, Osceola, WI 54020-0001 USA.

Library of Congress Cataloging-in-Publication Data Available

ISBN 0-7603-1205-2

**On the front cover:** A 1964 model 281 Peterbilt still earning its keep years after it rolled off the production line.

**On the frontispiece:** An embellished second-generation badge gets a final rinse. The factory did not fancy ostentationsly polished surfaces in the early postwar days.

**On the title page:** It is not unusual to encounter old Peterbilts still on the road, looking as good as if they were still in their prime, even though two or three decades have passed since they first entered service. Pictured on the previous spread, a 350 conventional, class of 1955. Captured at speed by the camera, the old workhorse is here seen on its way back to base. The daily routine includes delivering hay to local dairies and horse farms.

**On the table of contents page:** Breathing through its huge, 1,444 square inch radiator, a mighty 289—a model built between 1967 and 1986—a model built between 1967 and 1986—zooms past twilight desert secnery.

**On the back cover:** Part of a company fleet, these haulers are ready for action.

Printed in China

# Contents

*Introduction*
Class from '39                                      6

*Peterbilt history*
Five decades of progress
forges product of distinction                       8

*Peterbilt pioneer*
Rare survivor resurrected                          27

*Collectible Peterbilts*
Cavalcade of classics                              34

*Peterbilt*
On the road                                        73

*Peterbilt*
At the truck stop                                  80

*Peterbilt*
On the job                                         88

*Peterbilt*
At the show                                        99

*New-generation Peterbilts*
Modern mastodons                                  113

*Peterbilt nomenclature*
Production numbers and
model designations                                126

## *Introduction*

# Class from '39

The first three decades of the Twentieth Century were tumultuous ones for truck manufacturers. The era witnessed the birth of hundreds of makes. Inevitably, it was also an era of sudden death, with a majority soon fallen by the roadside.

Perhaps it is not a calamity that trucks with names like Old Hickory, Ruggles, and Clydesdale no longer traffic our roads. But the likes of the classics—REO, Diamond T, Sterling—are certainly missed.

Peterbilt celebrated its fiftieth anniversary in 1989; it is still a relatively young company. This is not to say that success was a foregone conclusion from the beginning. When the Peterbilt factory opened its doors in the spring of 1939, who would have thought it an opportune time to start a business? On the world scene, Hitler was not only talking tough, but building an army to back up his threats, all fueling speculation of pending doom. And by the time the fourth Peterbilt took to the road, in late September, Nazi tanks had only a few weeks earlier crossed the Polish border, an action marking the outbreak of world conflict.

Peterbilt persisted. From an early beginning, when oddities such as plywood-clad cab interiors were still part of the picture, to the present, with its striking anniversary model pushing aerodynamic efficiency to a new level, Peterbilt has managed to build a product with a most enviable reputation in the business.

It is a reputation often summarized in a single word, a word proclaimed not only by the company brochures, but more importantly, pronounced by a faithful following of customers as well. The word to describe Peterbilt is Class.

# Five decades of progress forges product of distinction

When the first Peterbilt emerged in 1939, the occasion did not mark the introduction of a brand new creation or untested quantity, totally lacking in heritage and tradition. On the contrary, sporting many of the features and components from the recently defunct Fageol truck line, the newcomer could claim the distinction of being the direct descendant of one of the nation's pioneer truck manufacturers.

The Fageol Motor Car Company dated back to 1915. The firm, located in Oakland, California, first built luxury automobiles as well as buses and trucks. By the end of World War I, the automobile had given way to its utilitarian counterparts.

As demand for the trucks increased, so did specialization. Thanks to its location, Fageol was

**Distant Peterbilt relatives**
*A Fageol from the early twenties, pictured on the opposite page. The unusual load of an airplane fuselage was sufficient cause to call out the photographer. To the left, an impressive row of heavy-duty workhorses—rolling on pneumatic tires, a feature arriving in 1924— represent the look of the big Fageols of the mid-twenties. Above, a restored 1929 Fageol Model 370.*

able to cater to the unique needs of the West Coast truckers, whose hauls were particularly long and grueling, covering endless desert plains and steep mountain passes. As a result, Fageol soon earned a reputation for being both rugged and reliable.

With its foothold on the West Coast secure, it was natural that Fageol began looking to expand into the lucrative East Coast market. The opportunity arrived in 1924, when American Car and Foundry Company offered a substantial annual fee for the rights to manufacture Fageols in the East. Based on the tentative agreement, Fageol invested in expansion of the Oakland facility, as well as a new factory in Kent, Ohio.

Regrettably, the agreement with American Car and Foundry was never consummated; Fageol was forced to file for bankruptcy in 1929. The deepening Depression also hurt Fageol, and in 1932 the company went into receivership. The Waukesha Motor Company and the Central Bank of Oakland assumed control of the operation.

In spite of Fageol's financial difficulties, the next six years saw continued production as well as the introduction of a number of new models. Unfortunately, the flurry of activity did not forestall the future. When Sterling Motors acquired the assets in November 1938, it was announced that production would cease at the end of the year.

T. A. Peterman was a man whose mind was set on expansion and opportunity rather than on depression and regression. Peterman, a lumber magnate from Tacoma, Washington, was the proprietor of an extensive logging

and sawmill operation as well as a number of factories manufacturing a variety of wood products. He purchased Fageol in April 1939, expressly for the purpose of developing a special project: a chain-driven logging truck. Two units were built, but neither proved successful.

The failure of the special logger was of no consequence; as it turned out, the conventional trucks emerging from the factory put Peterman firmly on the map. The trucks were named Peterbilt, a designation Peterman adopted from the brand name of the wooden doors manufactured by one of his companies.

Factory records state that fourteen trucks were shipped in 1939. This figure does not include one unit, a chassis-only, which was sold to a fire apparatus manufacturer on June 21, according to other sources. The first complete truck, the three-axle L-100, was delivered to the Beckley Brothers of Stockton, California, on August 2. The second unit was the first two-axle truck, the M-101, and was shipped on August 18, also going to Stockton, with a certain Pete Bordenave the recipient.

First-year production featured an egg-crate aluminum grille, similar in style to the type used on the last of the Fageols. A number of the subsequent units sported an exposed radiator, surrounded by an aluminum shell and protected by a bumper-mounted brush guard. It is thought that the former style was reserved for over-the-road trucks, while the latter was fitted to vehicles destined for heavy-duty work, such as logging. Success in the logging market helped push

**Fageols of the thirties show the way**
By 1935, left, Fageols had taken on the look that a few years hence would inspire the early Peterbilts. Above, this 1937 Fageol sports a cast-aluminum grille, much like the one used by Peterbilt from 1939 to 1941. A detail that did not make it beyond the transition was the characteristic row of louvers, an item that had graced the Fageol hood almost since the beginning.

**Founding father, first offspring**
*Sternfaced and rugged, like the trucks he built, Al Peterman, above, was the man who got Peterbilt rolling. Highly collectible today, early brochures, right, promoted the product in vivid color and glowing terms. Among the first crop of trucks, opposite, were these attractive 260s, photographed in the yard behind the Oakland plant before being sent off on their tour of duty.*

production for 1940 to eighty-two units.

The egg-crate grille was dropped, it is believed, in 1941—an exact date cannot be determined due to inconclusive factory records. The year saw the completion of eighty-nine units. Production fell in 1942, to a total of fifty-seven. In 1943 the figure was up again, reaching seventy-four, while 1944 saw a more substantial increase—

thanks to war-related government contracts—with 225 trucks delivered.

In 1945, production took another considerable jump to 324 units. Peterman, who had until then been actively involved in the company, succumbed to cancer.

Demand for the rugged Peterbilt product continued in 1946, with the number of trucks built rising to 349. The following year,

Peterman's widow sold the company's assets—excluding the land—to a group of Peterbilt management. At that time the corporate title, Peterman Manufacturing Company—of which the truck manufacturing firm had been a subsidiary—was changed to Peterbilt Motors Company.

With the emergence of the first postwar Peterbilts came subtle changes in appearance. While the

**The show takes to the road**
*A 260, above, typifies the first Peterbilts. Not typical is the equipage to the right, Peterbilt providing the kit for a Stutz fire truck rebuild. Note the combination of 260 bumper and headlights, and 270 radiator shell. Pictured on the opposite page, a row of heavy-duty 354 loggers—sporting wooden bumpers and skirtless fenders—and two 354 dump trucks.*

cab, hood, radiator shell and fenders stayed virtually unchanged over the next few years, the bumper was the subject of continuous experimentation. The earliest trucks sporting the egg-crate grille were fitted with a smoothly rounded bumper. Next came a utilitarian style, featuring a straight steel channel. In some cases the open end was turned outward and covered by a hardwood board. Later,

an all-steel bumper came into use. This was characterized by a row of four round holes, allowing increased airflow to the radiator. Finally this style was replaced by a type sporting four horizontal slots in place of the holes.

Peterbilt's manufacturing level remained stable throughout 1948, with the total settling on 316 units for the year. In 1949, the company experienced a steep decline in

production and only 214 trucks were assembled.

Major revisions to the product line came in 1949. The frontal aspect took on a new appearance, sporting a narrower, lower bumper that exposed more of the radiator and resulted in a taller look—The New Look. It was a style that would characterize Peterbilts for years to come. Also contributing to the new facial expression, the headlamps were moved from the fenders to brackets protruding from each side of the radiator.

In 1950, Peterbilt unveiled its first cabover: the 280/350, a model remaining in production for five years. Another milestone was passed in 1956: the second-generation cabover, the 281/351. Also that year, one more Peterbilt classic took to the road, the 281/351 conventional.

**In the beginning
the word was written**

*Above, the first Peterbilt badge, a style lasting only a few years. Company lore has it that the logo was derived from a sketch Peterman executed on a napkin during a dinner meeting. Left and opposite, two examples of pioneer Peterbilts from the 1940 to 1941 period, still wearing the earliest badge. Note the non-typical louvers on the side of the hood.*

**Legacy of a lumberman**
The founder thought it proper to fit his trucks with plywood interiors—after all, Peterman also owned a plywood manufacturing plant. The idea was soon abandoned, however, and the plywood interior is found only in the earliest trucks, above. Opposite page, as a result of Peterman's connections in the logging industry, many a Peterbilt was destined for a rugged life in the woods.

With the arrival of the new models came further acceptance of the Peterbilt product. Total output for the fifties exceeded 4,500 units. In comparison, total production for the forties was just over 2,000.

In the late fifties, Peterman's widow, who still owned the land on which the Peterbilt factory was built, announced her intention to sell out to a shopping center developer. This meant that Peterbilt was faced with the need to raise capital for a new factory, a daunting task for the aging owner team.

A buyer was found in Pacific Car and Foundry, an organization which also traced its beginnings to the infant years of the Twentieth Century, with steel milling and foundry operations forming the roots. Early efforts catered to the logging industry in the Pacific

### Badge of a new generation

The engineering drawing for the second badge, placing the script on a rectangular base, is dated November 2, 1944. Above, stark in its monochromatic austerity, the badge decorates the radiator of an unrestored survivor. Attached to the bumper, right, the badge brands one of a special series of Navy dump trucks. Opposite, two more trucks stand ready for delivery. Bottom, a 344 sports the new badge.

Northwest, and logging trucks and railroad cars became a mainstay. Later, after the outbreak of World War I, railroad boxcars were added to the manufacturing menu.

Between the wars, Pacific Car and Foundry expanded its product line to include buses and trolleys. With the onset of World War II, part of the capacity was switched to the production of Sherman tanks. Government contracts continued in the postwar era, with the development and manufacture of self-propelled guns.

With headquarters in Renton, Washington, Pacific Car and Foundry updated its name in 1972 to PACCAR, an appellation reflecting the modern aspects of a multi-national organization. Today there are manufacturing facilities in five countries on three continents, and the network of dealers and

representatives reaches into more than eighty nations. At the time of the June 1958 acquisition of Peterbilt, PACCAR was no newcomer to truck manufacture; venerable Kenworth had been added to the roster in 1945.

Backed by PACCAR, Peterbilt was able to obtain the capital needed for expansion and a new factory was built in Newark, a city located just south of Oakland, where production was in full swing by late 1960. With increased capacity the rate of production rose rapidly, and the total for the sixties was 21,000 units.

In 1969 a second manufacturing facility came on line. Located in Nashville, Tennessee, this plant opened new markets for Peterbilt, reflected in further

## Details of progress

Two examples of the first postwar generation, opposite, easily identified through subtle differences between the bumpers. The early truck sports four holes while the latter features four horizontal slots. Harnessed under the hood, above, potent Hall-Scott power. Left, the late forties saw the arrival of a new generation of Peterbilts, characterized by the tall radiator, here on a 280.

production increases. The total number of trucks built jumped to 72,000 units in the seventies.

In 1980 a third plant, located in Denton, Texas, added still more capacity. Manufacturing at the Newark facility was discontinued in 1986 although management, engineering and development remained. Still, total production for the eighties will surpass the 100,000 mark.

Five decades of progress has brought Peterbilt a long way, a reality illustrated by production figures that swelled from one truck per week to seventy a day. This feat is all the more remarkable since it was accomplished without compromising the original appeal, that certain blend of ruggedness and sophistication.

**Enter the oval**
The drawing for the third type of Peterbilt badge is dated February 16, 1953. Most company old-timers, however, state that it was executed after the fact, and it is assumed that the classic oval took its place on the radiator some time in 1951, above. Opposite, the new badge decorates a 350, and right, a 381. The 381 is a model illustrating Peterbilt's continued appeal in the heavy-duty field.

## *Peterbilt pioneer*

# Rare survivor resurrected

For years, old trucks have been thoroughly neglected, relegated to junkyards, or—in the best of times—used for occasional hauls by languishing trucking operations. Only a few enthusiasts were collecting the beat-up dinosaurs, always out of pure attraction for the breed, never for monetary gain.

While the cream of the classic automobiles of the twenties and thirties—the Cadillacs, Duesenbergs, and Packards—attracted the eye of the connoisseur early on, it took the test of time to elevate the cars of the forties and fifties to collector status. Now it is the turn of the muscle cars of the sixties and early seventies.

With today's established car collector market, prices have gone through the roof. But other objects are still within reach of the enthusiast limited by a slim pocketbook. This fact has collaborated with a latent passion to fuel today's interest in tractors and trucks. With the trend continuing and spreading to all types of rolling machinery, there is no telling where the avalanche will stop. Are forklifts next?

As with all collecting, the early, unique and hard-to-find are the most desirable. Featured on this and the following pages is an example of the first-generation Peterbilt. This survivor, chassis number L-119, is one of the oldest known Peterbilts, and has been restored to the most exacting standards by the manufacturer itself. The handsome specimen stands as a tribute to the ingenuity and patience of all true enthusiasts—those of fifty years ago, and those of today.

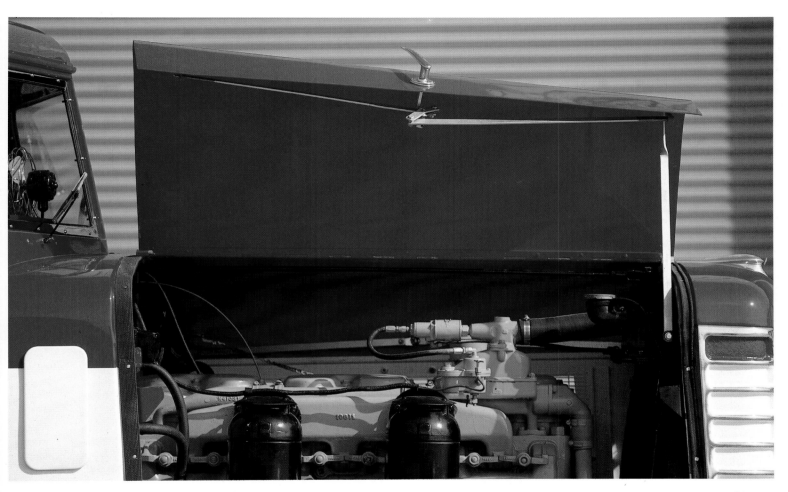

The truck pictured on this and the previous spread represents one of the most thorough restorations bestowed on a classic Peterbilt. Delivered on April 3, 1940, to C. J. Painter in Missoula, Montana—where it remained for nearly five decades—the survivor was brought back to its original state by the original maker, who relied on the skills of Jim Kliment and his crew at the Newark, California, test engineering facility. The frontal view, left, is dominated by the grille, a fragile piece of aluminum casting. The original Dietz headlights had been lost. A nationwide search produced a replacement set from a Massachusetts collector. The bumper, also missing, had to be manufactured from scratch, a task made easier as the original drawings were still in the Peterbilt archives. Above, the engine—a Cummins diesel, giving off 150 hp at 1800 rpm—has been restored to the correct HB specifications, although sporting a late forties HR block.

Pictured on the previous spread, the anniversary object in all its splendor, complete with Reliance stake bed and Goodyear-shod Budd wheels. On this spread, above, a closeup of the driver's environment. The doors and the interior of the cab were originally covered with a type of marine plywood that is no longer manufactured. For the restoration, the correct look was achieved by sectioning fur plywood into veneer-thin sheets. The dash—flat on the earliest models, table style on later ones—was manufactured from steel and decorated with painted-on wood grain, all according to original specifications. The battery of pull switches attached to the dash activates lights, fuel tanks, and heater and defroster fans. The T-handle mounted below the dash operates the engine compression release. The braided leather strap, in classic fashion, activates the air horn. The directional semaphore, right, is hand actuated. This early type sported reflectors only, while later styles were equipped with lights.

## Collectible Peterbilts

# Cavalcade of classics

The first few years of Peterbilt production were tough ones for the young company, its growth hampered by a lack of raw material due to the war. As the conflict neared its end, Peterbilt's struggle was eased by orders from the military. Still, only a few hundred units emerged from this, the first period.

With peace arrived an era of optimism. Peterbilt was finally able to expand its operation, but only on the West Coast. Most orders came from the California trucking capitals, such as Stockton and Fresno, strategically located on the route between Sacramento and Los Angeles. Another source of business was the logging industry in northern California and Oregon, where the ruggedness of the Peterbilt was much appreciated.

Throughout the remainder of the forties—the second period—Peterbilt production remained stable, with the rate resting at about one unit per day. Then, in the early fifties—the third period—new models were introduced. As these began attracting widening circles of customers—a trend aided by an increasing number of dealers—production rose.

Peterbilts manufactured during these three periods are today's collectible classics. Although some of the seemingly indestructible machines are still in active use, an increasing number are being restored and put away for posterity—intriguing mementos of the nation's early years of trucking and truck manufacture.

Pictured on this and the previous spread, another first-generation Peterbilt—a 1940 Model 260, serial number M-179—residing in the A. W. Hays truck museum, Woodland, California. Hays was among the first to own a Peterbilt. His check for $7,350 paid for L-101, delivered on September 30, 1939. Hays operated the truck for a decade before selling it. Years later, when he became interested in collecting, he had to be content with M-179, found in an Oakland junkyard. The condition of the truck was such that the restoration required the remanufacture of a number of parts, the bumper being one such item. In the process, the restorers overlooked drilling a hole for the hand crank. Liberty was also taken with original specifications in that the cab was replaced with one of a newer vintage; the earliest Peterbilts had the ventilators located on each side of the cowl, not on top. Above, M-179 still sports its early Cummins engine. To the right, wheels, fenders, badge and grille are all original.

The truck pictured on the previous spread is a curious specimen, although representative of its era. The rig—registered in 1941—is only partially a Peterbilt, the factory having provided a kit for the rebuilding of an aging Fageol. This procedure became popular during the war as production was concentrated on armaments and old trucks were given a second chance. The fenders, including the headlights and their mounting brackets, as well as the cab, are Fageol leftovers. The radiator and the hood are standard Peterbilt fare. Pictured on this page, another unique truck, a one-off Peterbilt. Titled in 1945, this rig is today the property of the son of the original owner, who trucked parts to the Peterbilt factory and had the vehicle built to his specifications. Power comes from a Waukesha gasoline unit. Remaining in the family until the late sixties, the truck was subsequently sold. Recently returned, the sentimental reunion took two decades in coming.

41

It is said that old Peterbilts refuse to die, and the specimen pictured here is living proof. Loyal Stanley (is the secret perhaps partially in the owner's name?) still operates his 1946 Model 270 on a commercial basis. Six-hundred-mile roundtrips are not unusual. In order to better cope with today's highway speeds, the wheels—originally Budd steel discs—have been replaced. Also non-original is the air cleaner, as well as the exhaust stack and the fuel tanks. Under the hood hides a 335 Cummins from 1968; yesterday's power was also supplied by Cummins. Original running gear fare was a four-speed transmission with a three-speed auxiliary unit. Brakes were by Timken, operating on two or four wheels, and featuring 16 inch alloy drums. Stanley's old-timer still sports the original type of bumper with its characteristic row of four slots. The radiator carries the correct, second-generation Peterbilt badge, while the hood displays the incorrect, new style.

George and Jim Diamantine of Hayward, California—a city located just south of the old Peterbilt plant in Oakland, and just north of the present Newark headquarters—inherited this 1946 Model 354 heavy-duty dual-drive from their father, who bought it new. Part of a fleet of 16 trucks, the Peterbilt was initially used for transporting redwood from Booneville in northern California, to Hayward, where the family's lumberyard was located. Later, the truck was used for local delivery, at which time a bed was fitted. The workhorse remained in service until 1960. Nearly three decades later, the brothers decided to resurrect the old-timer. The premise of the restoration was admirable: every effort was made to respect the original specifications and avoid undue embellishments. The handsome survivor emerged as one of the best examples around of the early postwar Peterbilts. The Cummins 220 is from 1958, and thus non-original, as is the exterior air cleaner and oil filter.

The sparkling 270 Peterbilt pictured
on this spread stands as homage to the
staying power of a 43 year old Peterbilt
survivor and the skill of an 18 year old
truck enthusiast. Darin Beachler,
whose father and brother own a
trucking operation in Modesto,
California, bought the worn machine
for $3,500. Five months and thousands
of dollars later, the 1946 Peterbilt was
ready to return to the road. Beachler's
objective was not to build a show
truck—although his handiwork has
won him several trophies—but a
working machine. Therefore, the
restoration did not conform to original
specifications but endowed the truck
with the latest technology, such as a
new rear end, new wiring and air lines,
and a completely rebuilt 262 Cummins.
Stainless steel and chrome were used to
enhance bumpers, grille, running
boards, exhaust stacks and fuel tanks.
The interior received modern gauges,
and an air conditioning unit, smartly
hidden under the seat.

Factory documents reveal that this 355 heavy-duty dual-drive Peterbilt, serial number L-1205, was delivered to the Gilchrist Timber Company, Gilchrist, Oregon, on July 23, 1947. Today, this outstanding example of an early Peterbilt logger is the proud possession of Jack Campbell, Covelo, California. His restoration, aided by the skilled mechanics employed in his trucking business, put the truck back in exactly the condition it was when delivered four decades ago—with one exception. The wheels, like the frame and body, were originally Chinese Red. Campbell's choice of white for the wheels certainly sets them off nicely, as seen on the following spread. The classic Peterbilt logger—with all of its 271 inches of heavy-duty steel stretched against a proper background—cuts a most impressive profile. The original wheels were steel-disc Budds, while the original tires were Goodyear Road Lugs.

49

A heavy-duty logger demands heavy-duty power, and power was the name of the game of the Hall-Scott engines. Pictured here is the very unit originally fitted to the truck, a Series 400, producing 325 hp. The Hall-Scott, manufactured in Berkeley, California— a city neighboring Oakland—is a true classic. A descendent from the famous Liberty aircraft engine of World War I, the straight-six features such finery as a single overhead camshaft. During World War II, Hall-Scott's magnificent V–12 propelled the Navy's superfast air-sea rescue boats, adding further fame to the name. Old truckers talk with affection about the Hall-Scotts. The only negative comments concern fuel consumption of about 2½ mpg, and as a result, many a Hall-Scott was converted to run on less-expensive butane. The firm called it quits in the late fifties, but not before producing the awesome Series 6182. Equipped with a turbocharger, this machine pioneered horsepower figures in the 450 range.

The original Peterbilt Specification Assembly Sheet for this logger lists a number of special options unique to the type of vehicle, such as the skirtless fenders. A wooden cab-top platform, used during loading, was also installed, as were step brackets—items presently missing. As seen in the photograph above, the headlights received special shielding, as did the fuel tanks. Furthermore, a tow hook was installed on the left side, while the right side received a yoke. Underneath, the frame was doubled-up, enabling the vehicle to withstand the punishment administered by the severe conditions in the wintry woods. The seats, in stark contrast to all the heavy-duty equipment, were upholstered in sumptuous genuine leather. A heater and a defroster fan completed the driver's comfort requirements. As seen in the view to the left, the workplace is dominated by the huge, 22 inch steering wheel.

The truck pictured on this and the following two spreads is a 1948 Model 344 dual-drive, a handsomely restored example of the last of the second-generation Peterbilts. The period began in 1946 with the arrival of the first peacetime units and ended with the new model introduction in 1949. The featured survivor provided many years of faithful service in the employ of three owners before it was bought by the Teresi Trucking Company of Lodi, California. It was restored at Teresi, a project requiring the better part of two years. Today, its usefulness is not over. The pampered old-timer—with terminal foreman Gary Moorman its only authorized driver—in addition to representing the company at trucker's conventions and exhibits, also doubles as a back-up tow truck, and is quite a show stopper in either capacity. Originally powered by a 200 Cummins, the long hood now hides a 280 Cummins of early sixties vintage.

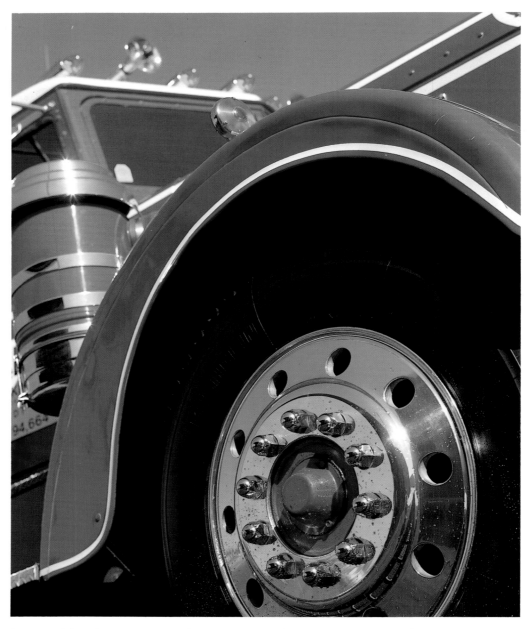

Executed for the purpose of show, the restoration of the Teresi Peterbilt called for embellishments beyond original specifications. The extra effort paid off, producing a most potent winner, as seen in the photograph to the right. In 1948, Peterbilts were still somewhat austere by today's standards. The roof of the cab, for instance, sported just one horn, mounted in the center, and lacked position lights altogether. Also non-original is the use of chrome on the radiator guard.

Furthermore, the early postwar Peterbilts were not fitted with exterior air cleaner and oil filter units, both decorative elements of the Teresi truck. The sheet metal, on the other hand, was untouched. The shape of the original-style fender, deep-skirted and pleasantly round, makes for an interesting photograph, above. The original steel-disc Budd wheels were painted, not polished. Here they were replaced by modern Alcoa aluminum discs.

Featured on this and the following spread, another curious Peterbilt. Starting life as a 1930 Fageol, the truck was rebuilt in 1948 using a Peterbilt factory kit. Exactly how much is Fageol and how much is Peterbilt would take extensive research to determine. The frame and cab are certainly by Fageol, just as sure as the radiator shell and hood are by Peterbilt. For a closer examination of the cab, compare the one pictured on this spread with the one shown on pages 38 and 39. Both trucks feature the original Fageol cab, updated with rubber-mounted windshield panes. The Fageol cab has a seamless frontal roofline; notice also the lack of drip molding. The conversion was the work of Connell Motor Truck Company. Connell is a name ringing with Peterbilt lore, as the firm, located in Stockton, California, was one of the earliest Peterbilt dealers and negotiated the sale of the first Peterbilt truck.

Pictured above, an interior view of
Connell Motor's tow truck. The dash is
a hand-me-down Fageol, the style
calling for a grouping of the
instruments in a cluster, centered on
the vertical board. The gauges located
in front of the steering wheel were
installed at the time of the conversion.
Curiously, symbolizing the
amalgamation of the two makes, the
foot pedals—unfortunately not
showing in the photograph—are of
different manufacture: the clutch pedal
carries the Fageol insignia, the
accelerator pedal features the Peterbilt
logo. Pictured on the opposite page, yet
another view of the second-generation
Peterbilt badge. The photograph also
calls attention to the radiator
ornament. There were subtle
differences with regards to this item.
The early design had a smoother curve,
conforming to the round first-
generation radiator shell, as well as a
longer tail. The new design follows the
shape of the new radiator shell, with
its sharper edges.

The 1950 introduction of Peterbilt's
first cabover design was a welcome
solution to growing problems facing
the truckers. With regulations limiting
the overall length of truck trains, the
cabover allowed for increased payload
space, promoting profitability. Pictured
here, a working specimen of a 1952
vintage. The two cabover models, a
two-axle and a three-axle, were, like
their conventional Peterbilt cousins,
designated 280/350. The cab could be
tilted forward but the procedure was
somewhat time consuming. The option
was used for major surgery and not—
as on Peterbilt's third-generation
cabover, the 282/352, introduced in
1959—for general service access.
Access to the 280/350 was through the
fenders, which were held in place by
cap screws and swung outward, and
also through the front panel, which
was hinged at the top, and swung
upward for easy access to the air
cleaner, as well as the fuel, oil and air
lines.

Peterbilt's 280/350 cabover, with its snub-nose frontal features and imposing height, is quite an eyeful. Measuring the distance from the ground to the top of the cab, the vehicle stands almost ten feet tall. Pictured on this spread, a 1954 survivor. Featured on the following spread, another Peterbilt classic, a 1955 Model 350 conventional. When introduced in 1949, in addition to the new radiator shell, relocation of the headlights and lowering of the bumper, the 280/350 conventionals featured a new hood and redesigned cab. Although built according to traditional Peterbilt style, the new cab was roomier and provided improved weather- and sound-proofing, with the firewall and toe boards insulated, and the rest of the cab lined. The featured trucks are owned and restored by Philip Troost of Mira Loma, California, an ardent collector of old machinery. Over the years, his sprawling backyard has taken on the intriguing qualities of both graveyard and museum.

## *Peterbilt*

# On the road

Unlike the best-trained marathon runners, who perform at abnormal levels, Peterbilt trucks run with complete ease, regardless of speed and distance. Running is what Peterbilts do best.

And just as running is natural for Peterbilts, the open road is their natural habitat.

Then what makes Peterbilts run?

Cummins power propelled the Peterbilts right from the start. While today's menu also offers the complete Caterpillar and Detroit Diesel ranges, the earliest models could be had with Waukesha gasoline units in addition to the Cummins diesels. For heavy-duty applications, such as logging, Hall-Scott's powerful gasoline engine was once the recommended fare.

For delivery of all that power to the road, Peterbilt chose only quality suppliers. Clutches, transmissions and driveshafts were by Spicer, axles and brakes by Timken, wheels by Budd and Dayton—just to mention a few of the classic industry names.

Ride and handling were always pet subjects of Peterbilt engineers. Early on, the company pioneered the application of a unique air suspension design. Today's trucks float on Peterbilt's patented Air Leaf system, featuring special tracking rods that improve both ride softness and roll stability.

The latest arena of innovation is aerodynamics, where Peterbilts can be had with roof fairings, cab-side extenders, and cab skirt fairings—all in addition to a special bumper featuring a smooth, wind-cheating shape.

No wonder Peterbilts love to run.

On the previous spread, Peterbilt's rugged 349 captured at speed on a rain drenched city freeway. This model, introduced in 1984, represents the firm's previous line of construction trucks, and was superseded by the 357 in 1986. Both designs feature slope-nose fiberglass hoods. The latter also comes in a super-heavy-duty version, featuring flat steel fenders and a butterfly steel hood. A host of engine options are offered, ranging from 250 to 444 hp. On this spread, two more Peterbilt front-runners, captured in pain and in pleasure. Above, a 362 cabover forges ahead in spite of appalling road conditions. Introduced in 1981, and still going strong, the 362 is available as a 63 inch non-sleeper, as well as in 90 and 110 inch sleeper configurations. Right, another example of one of Peterbilt's long-running favorites: a 359, captured during an easy-street, palm-escorted excursion. First available in 1967, the 359 was superseded by the 379 in 1986.

It is not unusual to encounter old Peterbilts still on the road, looking as good as if they were still in their prime, even though two or three decades have passed since they first entered service. Pictured on the previous spread, a 350 conventional, class of 1955. Captured at speed by the camera, the old workhorse is here seen on its way back to base. The daily routine includes delivering hay to local dairies and horse farms. Pictured on this spread, a 359 tanker, greeting the falling dusk with blazing lights. This Peterbilt classic—in spite of its square-hooded appearance—incorporates all the latest innovations, having been continuously updated during nearly two decades of production. When replaced by the 379 in 1986, the traditional look of the 359 was still not outdated, but was carried into the new generation—to the point where the uninitiated would be hard pressed to see the difference. Such is the staying power of a Peterbilt.

*Peterbilt*

# At the truck stop

It is past six. Supper time. The gas station signs, one by one, light up against the reddening California sky—the Chevron shield, the Union 76 ball, and on the other side of the freeway, the Shell shell. Further down the off-ramp, another sign flashes Truck Diesel in white letters on a blue background.

Richard Gardner steers his 1987 Peterbilt—a classic with 398,826 miles on the odometer—in between the rows of pumps. He is far from home, and hungry. Home is Nicholson, Mississippi. Hungry is carved out by the mental image of a salad with Blue Cheese dressing, a steak sandwich and a cup of coffee.

But first the truck. The Cat is thirsty. He pumps fifty gallons, then checks the oil and tires, all eighteen tires. A bolt is stuck in one of the outside ones on the left side of the rear axle. He moves the truck to the service area and orders the tire repaired while he eats. "Run the truck through the wash when you are done, will you?"

After supper, three refills of coffee and a phone call to Sandra, his wife, he heads out to the Peterbilt, washed now and ready for action.

But first a smoke. A Camel classic, sitting in the cab with the door open, looking up at the night sky, thinking.

The trailer is empty. A load of batteries delivered in Concord this afternoon, hauled all the way from New Orleans. On the way to Santa Maria now. Three-hour drive. A sleep in the sleeper. Loading produce in the morning, and then on back to Mississippi.

The picture on the previous spread, photographed at a truck stop along one of California's main arteries, bustling Highway 5, shows a 1988 Model 379. The truck glitters like a Christmas tree with its row of roof-mounted position lights. The twin gas tanks hold a total of 323 gallons. The load, Douglas Fir lumber, is an overnight delivery to a customer in Los Angeles. On this spread, Elwood Staley of Chipley, Florida, scribbles a few entries in the logbook before settling down behind the wheel of his 1987 Model 379 Peterbilt. Both are ready to continue their interrupted cross-country run. The fuel tanks, as well as the stomach, have been appropriately filled, and some additional provisions brought aboard in the paper sack at Staley's feet. Sharing life on the road forges a relationship between the Peterbilt and its driver that cuts right to the core of the concept of man and machine.

82

In our age the need for individual expression has expanded the boundaries of communication—beyond the black of Ford's Model T, beyond the flamboyant shades of the fifties, beyond the psychedelics of the sixties. Our era has become the era of the expression explosion—from subway graffiti to T-shirt slogans, from promotional hats to race cars plastered with manufacturer's advertising. Today, any and all products become vehicles for the expression of personal tastes. In this world, the Peterbilt logo holds its own and is carried with pride, whether the personal expression has a touch of the winsome, as in the picture above, or the awesome, as in the frontal aspect depicted on the opposite page. On the following spread, the wet, windswept parking lot of a truck stop has become a Peterbilt parade ground. With their gaping radiator openings, their ramrod bumpers and their towering exhaust stacks, these battleships of the highway express images of supremacy.

"BLACK GOLD"

Peterbilt

Peterbilt

Peterbilt

2086

NEVADA
34164 S

ORE.      P.U.C.
DNK 913

APPORTIONED
P109365
19 ILLINOIS 88

# *Peterbilt*

# On the job

Peterbilt has always prided itself on being able to cater to individual desires, offering a wide choice of models, features and components, all making it easy for the owner to tailor the truck to the specific needs of the job.

A Peterbilt brochure from 1955—a collector's item today—shows the many fields of possible application: powerful conventionals, pulling long freight trailers, posed against rugged mountain scenery and big sky desert landscapes; snub-nosed cabovers, hauling livestock or lumber, captured in front of city-scapes or cozy country settings; and off-highway giants, loaded with logs as large as the vehicles themselves, or pulling heavy bottom dumps filled with mountains of gravel.

Towards the end of this brochure, an action-packed illustration features the 381, a monstrous six-wheeler with setback front axle. The machine is pictured while being loaded with sugar cane, presumably on a plantation in Hawaii, the exotic destination for most of these unique creations.

In the seventies, another outrageous monster—the mixer and dump truck 346—was issued in a limited edition. This machine also featured six-wheel-drive. Gross vehicle weight was an impressive 59,000 pounds, a result of all the dimensions being oversized, readying the machine for its heavy-duty assignments.

Seen on the following pages are examples of some of the more down-to-earth models, captured in down-to-earth situations. A Peterbilt—no matter its age and shape—is always up to the job.

Pictured on the previous spread, Peterbilt's 357 construction truck—here fitted with massive flotation tires—shows off its formidable frontal aspect. An illustration of the adaptability of this model to a large variety of duties is found in the fact that the wheelbase option comes in a choice of one-inch increments. Special frame drilling, numerous end-of-frame options, air tank location options and exhaust mounting options further increase the customizing flexibility of

the 357. An important aspect of heavy-duty fitness is Peterbilt's special cab mounting system, acting as a buffer to both mechanical and human stress. In its ultimate form, the 357 can be had with six-wheel-drive. Pictured on this spread, above, a 1980 Model 359, engaged in hauling compressed automotive recyclables while on the opposite page, another 359 of 1979 vintage returns from delivering a load of logs to a plywood factory in Nevada.

Pictured on the previous spread, a
moderately updated 1955 Model 351
Peterbilt accepts a payload of dirt for
delivery to a construction site. The
charming workhorse—a collector's
item to some—is owned and operated
by Marian Waskiewich, a refugee from
Poland. Having arrived in the United
States only a few years ago, he already
enjoys the benefits of a free economic
system, driving his own truck and
creating his own opportunities.
Pictured on this spread, on the job for
some Peterbilts means having to
perform when others cannot. Here, a
1977 Model 359 tow truck—in pursuit
of a stranded motorist—carefully
makes its way across the slippery
surface of a winding mountain road,
made more hazardous by unexpected
snowfall. Pictured on the following
spread, a 351 workhorse from the early
sixties hauls a heavy load of sugar beets
in California's San Joaquin Valley.
When harvest time comes, the show is
always on—even as here, during the
early morning hours.

*Peterbilt*

# At the show

They used to be events exclusively for collectible automobiles of the classic persuasion, but no more. The show has become an accepted arena for beautiful trucks as well, although such get-togethers are not referred to as concours d'elegance or talked about in some other such fancy foreign terminology. A simple, straight-forward, all-American truck show will do.

It all illustrates the emergence of the truck as an object worthy of admiration. The vivid colors, the mirror-bright expanses of chrome, the spotless rubber surfaces, all appear just as enticing as those of the automobiles, but the scale is larger. The radiators open wider, the tires stand taller. And everywhere, lights shine bright, air horns extend sleek trumpets, metallic paint glitters in the sunlight, stripes and curlicues abound.

As for the owners—enthusiasts of both sexes— they display the same devotion as their automotive counterparts. Polishing rags flutter across animated reflections, toothbrushes scour hard-to-reach spots. And the spectator crowds are just as enthusiastic, although tight-fitting blue jeans and wide-brimmed cowboy hats are preferred over creations from Europe's fashion capitals.

Classification and judging is becoming increasingly sophisticated, with specific categories for various vintages of trucks as well as for in-use or off-the-road historic vehicles. In all this, Peterbilt occupies a place of honor.

For an aspiring truck driver, like the young man captured in the scene on the previous spread, stopped in awe before the enormity of the machine, a truck show is truly a place of inspiration. The object of the budding enthusiast's admiration constitutes yet another example of the Peterbilt appeal; not even a brutally wrecked specimen can be left to the oblivion of the junkyard. Seen in this photograph is Jim Botelho's labor of love. He took what was left of a totaled 1988 Model 379, replaced the drivetrain and engine, adding potent power in the form of Caterpillar's 425 hp 3406 B unit in the process. Two months of patience, paint and polish rendered the resurrected machine ready for the road—and the show. On this spread, above, the bright colors and blinking lights of truck show merriment is reflected in a Peterbilt's polished radiator shell. On the opposite page, the swank artistry of the Peterbilt badge is contrasted with the geometric austerity of a straight row of rivets.

Captured here, the look that excites. A personification of might and muscle is found in the frontal aspect of the sixties era Peterbilts, exemplified by a 1966 Model 281. The pampered rig is also the personification of pride and passion. The pride is derived from making a good living, from being one's own boss; the passion is for things well done. On weekdays, Orlando "Gomez" Meza, owner and operator of this combination collector's item and workhorse, administers harsh punishment to the not-so-young machine, hauling tomatoes, beets, grapes and apricots out of the muddy fields and dusty orchards of California's San Joaquin Valley. But on Saturday, he gives his bread-winner a rest, bath and polish. And on Sunday he takes it to the show. In this scene, while awaiting the judge's decision, Gomez reflects on the advantages of the young— personified by his daughter—where a life of no work and all play still earns the reward of an ice cream.

Pictures of polished perfection. The photographs on this spread display details of various accessory components, all illustrating the owner's attention to detail and the length to which they are willing to go in their quest for perfection. On the opposite page, the rear-wheel quarter fender of a seventies Peterbilt. The reflection in the mirror finish is the red back side of the cab. The rubber flap—decorated with the Peterbilt logo—improves the seal between the fender and the trailer, preventing dirt from being thrown up on the back of the cab. On this page, the accessory box of an eighties Peterbilt with its contents: emergency reflection triangles, flashlight and toolbox. The bat, manufactured from aluminum and also adorned with the Peterbilt logo, is not a promotional gimmick, nor a baseball fan's companion to the ballgame, but a useful tool. While whacking a tire, the driver compares the sound and can determine whether the volume of air in one unit matches another.

The two rigs pictured on the previous spread—together representing an investment of nearly a quarter of a million dollars—exemplify the new-generation Peterbilt conventional in its most advanced form. Not only painted the same metallic blue but also sharing the same set of specifications, this pair of 377s are identical twins. Both feature Peterbilt's state-of-the-art roof fairing, as well as its most luxurious sleeper box, the 63 inch walk-through version. In addition, both are powered by Caterpillar's potent Model 3406. Here, the handsome pair is captured at play at a truck show in Santa Nella, California, surrounded by their drivers, Dan Reeves and Daniel Gomez, and their respective family members. At work, the trucks have to be satisfied with a decidedly more unglamorous lifestyle, ferrying restaurant produce to Los Angeles and San Francisco. On this spread, Tracy Allen and Paul Silvera admire the exquisite frontal features of a 1969 Model 351 Peterbilt.

108

Catching late luminous light, on the opposite page, is a row of Peterbilt cabovers, decorative in their flowing two-tone livery. A pristine specimen of the 362 occupies center stage. Flanking this machine are two well-preserved examples of the 352, a design introduced in 1959. After a decade, this long-running favorite received a redesigned cab, called the Pacemaker, and kept on trucking for another decade. The 362 arrived on the scene in 1981 and is still a popular member of the Peterbilt team. Note its one-piece windshield—giving an unobstructed panoramic view of the road scenery— and the triple set of wipers, ready and able to handle its janitorial assignment. Above, the imposing grille of a 379. Standard style features three vertical bars. Here the owner has fitted an additional four, the personal touch. The winged hood ornament—made from aluminum—doubles as a handle and came into use with the 1965 introduction of the tilt hood.

## New-generation Peterbilts

# Modern mastodons

The late fifties saw Peterbilt's production double and two units emerged from the Oakland facility each day in 1959. In the sixties, with the Newark plant on line, the figure increased many times over; by 1969, daily output surpassed ten units. In the seventies, as the Tennessee and Texas plants added further capacity—and an ability to support a national dealer network—the figure rose even more dramatically.

Altogether, fifty years of continuous Peterbilt production has placed nearly 200,000 trucks on the road. With the first two decades accounting for as few as some 6,500 units, the potential for collectibility of the early Peterbilts becomes obvious.

But where are they all? Still on the road! At least a great many of them. And certainly the ones of later vintage.

In contrast to an automobile, which is dramatically sensitive to fashion fluctuations, a truck can stay competitive for decades—although with aerodynamics becoming such a force in truck design, this will change. Thus, for the time being, a well-maintained Peterbilt from the sixties is far from out of the running. In fact, it often takes a trained eye to spot the differences.

All through the years, Peterbilt has maintained a position on the cutting edge of technology. This is also true with today's product line, which spans a spectrum including anything a trucker may desire, from the classic 379 conventional, long-nosed and impressively powerful, to the brand new 372 cabover, designed to master the wind.

Pictured on the previous spread, a brand new specimen of Peterbilt's versatile 378. Set apart visually from its 379 colleague, which sports a virtually horizontal hood made of aluminum, the 378 features a gently sloping hood made of fiberglass. The impressive adaptability of this Peterbilt model manifests itself in its multitude of options. For instance, front axle settings: in addition to the standard setting, a 46 inch setback position is offered. The latter option was chosen for the pictured truck, and results in optimal weight transfer, allowing for bigger payloads. Pictured on this spread, left, a shiny new 377. Above, a 300 hp Caterpillar fills the engine compartment of a 1987 cement mixer with a veritable snake's nest of pipes, tubes and hoses.

Pictured on this and the previous spread, Peterbilt's entry in the conventional streamliner category, the handsome, high-performance 377, introduced in 1986. Although pleasing to the eye, the good looks are not the major selling point of this popular Peterbilt. The bottom line is profitability. With almost half of today's operating expenses contributable to fuel, aerodynamics has become the latest weapon in the battle against rising costs. The beauty lies in the fact that the savings can be gleaned without a loss of power. As with other Peterbilts, the 377 can be had with a setback front axle. The featured specimen, a 1988 model fancifully painted and optimally equipped all to the specifications of a fast food chain, illustrates the standard axle configuration. Under the smoothly sloping fiberglass hood featuring forward tilt capability, hides the top-of-the-line 444 Cummins. Inside the cab, the UltraRide seats and futuristic wraparound dash caters to the driver's comfort needs.

Posed against the contrasting bright blue of the sky, as pictured in the photograph on the previous spread, and painted in Peterbilt's 50th anniversary color scheme of white and maroon—and dressed up further with luxurious gold striping—this 1989 Model 379 was specially prepared by Peterbilt for hauling the company's anniversary exhibit on promotional tours around the nation. Like a limited number of special anniversary edition trucks, made available for sale through dealers during the 1989 anniversary year, this particular specimen has its Peterbilt badge accented in gold tone, as seen in the photograph above, rather than in the conventional silver configuration. Pictured on the opposite page, Peterbilt's anniversary logo— with its subtle, elegant design— illustrates better than words the class of a company that has placed as many as 200,000 trucks on the road during its 50 years of operation.

After applying aerodynamics to the styling of the conventional truck, Peterbilt next tackled the cabover. Pictured on this spread, the latest creation to emerge from the Peterbilt engineers: the 372, a design pushing the application of aerodynamics several strides forward. Above, a photograph of the scale model, which was put through wind-tunnel testing before its shape was transferred to a full-scale running prototype. After thorough on-road testing, a batch of full-scale pilot units were completed. These units were built to prepare the new design for the production line. One of these pre-production pilots is seen in the photograph on the opposite page. Note that the sunshade also functions as a drag-reducing airfoil—a revolutionary design feature—and that the roof fairing has become an integral part of the body. This innovation results in exceptional cabin roominess, and allows a six-foot, one-inch individual the luxury of being able to stand up straight in front of the passenger seat.

*Peterbilt nomenclature*

# Production numbers and model designations

The following information reflects the level of knowledge at the time of publication. Therefore, as it concerns the early years of Peterbilt history in particular—a period of incomplete record keeping—the figures given below may not necessarily constitute the final word. The year of production is followed by the site of the factory.

| Year | Newark |
|---|---|
| 1960 | 812 |
| 1961 | 818 |
| 1962 | 1,080 |
| 1963 | 1,450 |
| 1964 | 1,800 |
| 1965 | 2,350 |
| 1966 | 2,720 |
| 1967 | 2,430 |
| 1968 | 3,450 |
| 1969 | 4,095 |

| Year | Nashville | Newark | Total |
|---|---|---|---|
| 1970 | 684 | 2,512 | 3,196 |
| 1971 | 1,663 | 3,105 | 4,768 |
| 1972 | 2,374 | 3,532 | 5,906 |
| 1973 | 2,659 | 5,117 | 7,776 |
| 1974 | 4,450 | 4,999 | 9,449 |
| 1975 | 1,535 | 1,798 | 3,333 |
| 1976 | 3,263 | 3,945 | 7,208 |
| 1977 | 5,714 | 5,536 | 11,250 |
| 1978 | 6,255 | 3,208 | 9,463 |
| 1979 | 4,184 | 5,509 | 9,693 |

| Year | Oakland | Year | Oakland |
|---|---|---|---|
| 1939 | 14 | 1950 | 340 |
| 1940 | 82 | 1951 | 368 |
| 1941 | 89 | 1952 | 411 |
| 1942 | 57 | 1953 | 321 |
| 1943 | 74 | 1954 | 276 |
| 1944 | 225 | 1955 | 480 |
| 1945 | 324 | 1956 | 649 |
| 1946 | 349 | 1957 | 491 |
| 1947 | 313 | 1958 | 400 |
| 1948 | 316 | 1959 | 777 |
| 1949 | 214 | | |

| Year | Total | Year | Total |
|---|---|---|---|
| 1980 | 6,964 | 1985 | 11,521 |
| 1981 | 7,505 | 1986 | 10,599 |
| 1982 | 5,628 | 1987 | 14,219 |
| 1983 | 8,642 | 1988 | 17,500 |
| 1984 | 14,911 | | |

Grand total 1939-88: 197,086

| Model | Year of intro | Comments |
|---|---|---|
| 120 Conventional | 1939 | Two-axle, chassis only |
| 260 Conventional | 1939 | Two-axle, chain-drive |
| 334 Conventional | 1939 | Three-axle, enclosed-drive |
| 270 Conventional | 1942 | Two-axle, enclosed-drive |
| 344 Conventional | 1942 | |
| 345 Conventional | 1942 | |
| 354 Conventional | 1942 | Heavy-duty |
| 355 Conventional | 1942 | Heavy-duty |
| 280/350 Conventional | 1949 | |
| 380 Conventional | 1949 | |
| 280/350 Cabover | 1950 | |
| 360 Conventional | 1950 | |
| 370 Conventional | 1950 | Heavy-duty |
| 390 Conventional | 1950 | Heavy-duty |
| 281/351 Conventional | 1954 | Lightweight |
| 381 Conventional | 1954 | Off-highway |
| 281/351 Cabover | 1956 | |
| 356 Cabover | 1956 | |
| 364 Conventional | 1956 | |
| 371 Conventional | 1956 | |
| 451 Cabover | 1956 | Four-axle |
| 282/352 Cabover | 1959 | Tilt cab |
| 287 Cabover | 1961 | Fifty-inch cab |
| 283 Conventional | 1961 | Setback axle |
| 383 Conventional | 1961 | Off-highway |
| 341 Conventional | 1962 | Mixer, dump |
| 343 Conventional | 1963 | Six-wheel-drive, no cab |
| 348 Conventional | 1963 | Mixer, dump |
| 358 Conventional | 1965 | Tilt hood |
| 288 Conventional | 1967 | Tilt hood |
| 289 Conventional | 1967 | Wide, tilt hood |
| 359 Conventional | 1967 | Wide, tilt hood |
| 200 Cabover | 1969 | Two-axle, LCF |
| 300 Cabover | 1969 | Three-axle, LCF |
| 346 Conventional | 1973 | Six-wheel-drive special |
| 353 Conventional | 1973 | Off-highway |
| 387 Conventional | 1974 | Off-highway |
| 310 Cabover | 1977 | LCF |
| 362 Cabover | 1981 | |
| 397 Conventional | 1982 | Heavy-duty off-highway |
| 349 Conventional | 1984 | Construction |
| 320 Cabover | 1985 | LCF |
| 357 Conventional | 1986 | Construction, fiberglass tilt hood |
| 375 Conventional | 1986 | Short haul, aerodynamic fiberglass tilt hood |
| 377 Conventional | 1986 | Long haul, aerodynamic fiberglass tilt hood |
| 379 Conventional | 1986 | Long haul, aluminum tilt hood |
| 376 Conventional | 1987 | Short haul, aerodynamic fiberglass tilt hood |
| 378 Conventional | 1987 | Medium to long haul, fiberglass tilt hood |
| 13-210 Mid Ranger | 1987 | Intra-city delivery |
| 357 Conventional | 1988 | Construction, steel/aluminum butterfly hood |
| 372 Cabover | 1988 | Aerodynamic |

**Peterbilts on parade.**
*Pictured in the illustration on the opposite page, an impressive row of Peterbilt cement mixers—thirteen to be exact. The era is the immediate postwar, the model is the dual-drive 345. Note the slotted bumpers. Pictured above, the Model 351, introduced in 1954—a perennial Peterbilt favorite. Note in this photo the relatively inconspicuous bumper, now featuring two rectangular openings.*

The author wishes to thank Peterbilt Motors Company for its assistance during the work's research phase, and for supplying the book's selection of historic photographs. Special thanks go to Sam Brown, Chris Cavette, Hap Furiya, Dave Hollar, Ed Klar, Jim Kliment and Dick Sherrard, all of Peterbilt. Furthermore, in addition to the owners listed in the captions throughout the book, Jim Edsberg (pages 38 and 39), Henry Ellery (page 9), Bob Senna (pages 40 and 41) and Marilyn Wright (pages 110 and 111) graciously allowed their trucks to be photographed. Walter Simonds, regional vice president of the American Truck Historical Society, deserves particular recognition for providing invaluable leads to surviving old-timers. Also contributing to the book with assistance and information were Louie Asborno, John Augustine, Jenny Bruinsma, A. W. Hays, Bob Howze, Homer Kerr, Al Manasse, Ron Mlakar, Rick McHugh, Robbie Rister, John Teresi and Jim Wood.